Follow Me Around™

France

By Wiley Blevins

SCHOLASTIC

Content Consultant:
Brett Bowles, PhD
Director of the Institute for European Studies
Indiana University—Bloomington
Bloomington, Indiana

Library of Congress Cataloging-in-Publication Data
Names: Blevins, Wiley, author.
Title: France / by Wiley Blevins.
Description: New York, NY : Children's Press, an imprint of Scholastic Inc., 2019. | Series: Follow me around | Includes bibliographical references and index.
Identifiers: LCCN 2017060412 | ISBN 9780531129234 (library binding) | ISBN 9780531138656 (pbk.)
Subjects: LCSH: France—Juvenile literature. | France—Description and travel—Juvenile literature.
Classification: LCC DC17 .B59 2019 | DDC 944—dc23
LC record available at https://lccn.loc.gov/2017060412

Design: Judith Christ Lafond & Anna Tunick Tabachnik
Text: Wiley Blevins

Printed in North Mankato, MN, USA 113

Scholastic Inc., 557 Broadway, New York, NY 10012

1 2 3 4 5 6 7 8 9 10 R 28 27 26 25 24 23 22 21 20 19

Photos ©: cover background: Brian Kinney/Shutterstock; cover children: Maria Teijeiro/Getty Images; back cover: Maria Teijeiro/Getty Images; 3: aronaze/iStockphoto; 4 background: Brian Jannsen/Alamy Images; 4 children: Maria Teijeiro/Getty Images; 6 left: FOTOSEARCH RM/age fotostock; 6 right: leoks/Shutterstock; 7 top left: Barry Mason/Alamy Images; 7 bottom left: EQRoy/Shutterstock; 7 right: LOOK Die Bildagentur der Fotografen GmbH/Alamy Images; 8 left: Ghislain & Marie David de Lossy/iStockphoto; 8 Pain au chocolat: Rixie/Dreamstime; 8 Croissant: chaosmaker/iStockphoto; 8 Baguette: aronaze/iStockphoto; 9 top: Premier Photo/Shutterstock; 9 center top: LauriPatterson/iStockphoto; 9 center bottom: Buretsu/iStockphoto; 9 bottom: Eurngkwan/iStockphoto; 10: BERTRAND LANGLOIS/AFP/Getty Images; 11: JOHN KELLERMAN/Alamy Images; 12 top: Tomacco/iStockphoto; 12 bottom left: Iaremenko Sergii/Shutterstock; 12 bottom right: eduardrobert/iStockphoto; 12-13 background: Vadim Yerofeyev/Dreamstime; 13 right: AF Fotografie/Alamy Images; 14 center: Consu1961/iStockphoto; 14 right: Fine Art Images/Getty Images; 14 left: Laesperanza/iStockphoto; 15 top center: Tono Balaguer/age fotostock; 15 top left: Pawel Libera/Getty Images; 15 top right: AlexKozlov/iStockphoto; 15 bottom: Steve Cadman/Flickr; 16 left: Jose Ignacio Soto/Shutterstock; 16 right: beatrice preve/Alamy Images; 17 top right: ANDREYGUDKOV/iStockphoto; 17 top left: P. Royer/age fotostock; 17 bottom: Le Do/Shutterstock; 18 left: North Wind Picture Archives/Alamy Images; 18 center left: Sarin Images/The Granger Collection; 18 center right: Albrecht Durer/Sarin Images/The Granger Collection; 18 right: North Wind Picture Archives/Alamy Images; 19 left: Jacques Louis David/The Granger Collection; 19 right: Naga Film/Getty ImagesGetty Images; 20 top left: TIMOTHY A. CLARY/AFP/Getty Images; 20 top right: Wolf Gang/Flickr; 20 bottom left: Victor VIRGILE/Gamma-Rapho/Getty Images; 20 bottom center: Francois Durand/Getty Images; 20 bottom right: Pascal Le Segretain/Getty Images; 21 top left: Christianm/Dreamstime; 21 bottom: nikonaft/iStockphoto; 21 top right: gangliu10/iStockphotoiStockphoto; 22 left: nito/Shutterstock; 22 top right: Rebecca Sager/www.beccasagerphoto.com; 22 bottom right: Rebecca Sager/www.beccasagerphoto.com; 23 top left: Marielle, Bruno/Getty Images; 23 center left top: Alexander Sandvoss/age fotostock/; 23 center left bottom: Christina McWilliams/Shutterstock; 23 bottom left: PHILIPPE HUGUEN/AFP/Getty Images; 23 right: Rebecca Sager/www.beccasagerphoto.com; 24 top left: Franck CRUSIAUX/Gamma-Rapho/Getty Images; 24 top right: Chris Graythen/Getty Images; 24 bottom: braverabbit/iStockphoto; 25 left: Poznyakov/Shutterstock; 25 right: John Elk III/Getty Images; 26 bottom left: Utekhina Anna/Shutterstock; 26 top left: Steve Debenport/Getty Images; 26 top right: Album/; 26 bottom right: Panoramic Images/Getty Images; 27 top left: mrs/Getty Images; 27 top right: kodachrome25/Getty Images; 27 center right: mchudo/iStockphoto; 27 bottom left: ariwasabi/iStockphoto; 27 bottom right: Morgan Hank/Getty Images; 28 A: Tim Oram/age fotostock; 28 B: Petroos/iStockphoto; 28 G: The Granger Collection; 28 C: Jorisvo/iStockphoto; 28 D: guy-ozenne/iStockphoto; 28 E: Ferrero-Labat/ard/age fotostock; 28 F: chris-mueller/iStockphoto; 30 top right: chokkicx/iStockphoto; 30 top left: Leontura/iStockphoto; 30 bottom: Maria Teijeiro/Getty Images.

Maps by Jim McMahon/Mapman ®.

Table of Contents

Where in the World Is France?

Bonjour (bon-JOOR) from France! That's how we say "hello." I'm Hugo (YOO-goh), and this is my *amie* (ah-MEE), or friend, Chloë. We welcome you to our beautiful and fashionable country. France is located in western Europe. Our country is sometimes called "the Hexagon" because of its unique six-sided shape. France is divided into 13 regions. There are a lot of interesting places to see. Ready? Let's get going!

USA

FRANCE

Fast Facts:

- France covers 212,935 square miles (551,500 square kilometers) in Europe.
- Spain, Andorra, and Monaco lie south of France. Italy and Switzerland are to the east. Germany, Luxembourg, and Belgium are to the northeast. The United Kingdom lies across the English Channel.
- The island of Corsica in the Mediterranean Sea is part of France.
- France's main rivers are the Loire, Seine, Garonne, and Rhône.
- Mountain ranges include the French Alps and the Pyrenees.

Nearly everyone in Paris lives in an apartment.
Some villages have buildings that are centuries old.

Home Sweet Home

We are from Paris, France. Families here are usually small and close-knit. We both come from families with two kids, and each of us has a sister. We both live in the same apartment building, along with some of our other friends from school.

We often spend holidays and weekends in a village outside Paris. There, each of our families shares a house with grandparents, aunts, uncles, and cousins. It's always fun when we get to see them! It's a full house when we are all there at the same time.

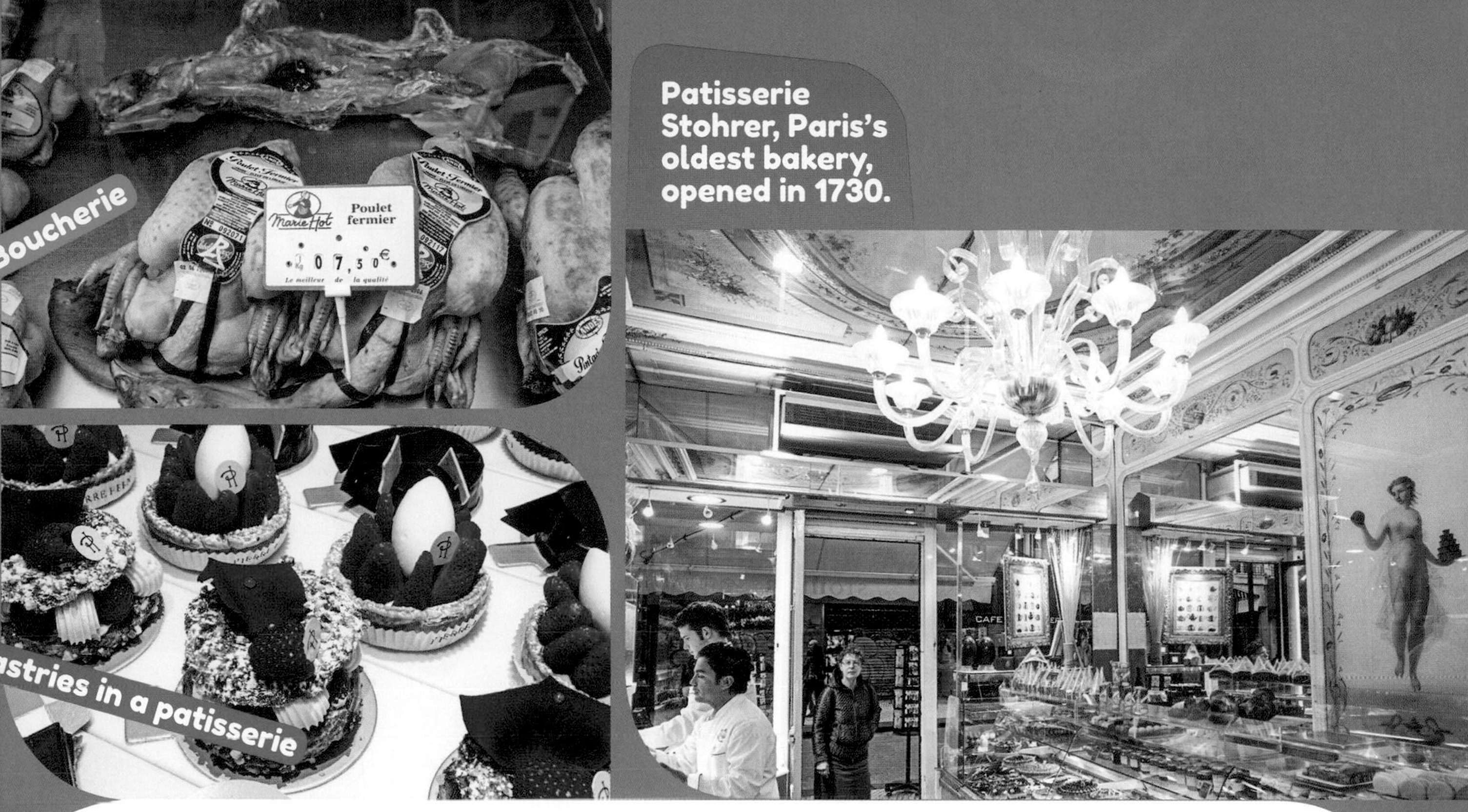

Boucherie

Pastries in a patisserie

Patisserie Stohrer, Paris's oldest bakery, opened in 1730.

Ours is just one of the villages that dot France's countryside. Each town is organized around a village square. A church or town hall usually stands in the square. It is fun for us to roam the narrow village streets when we visit. We love to see all the old stone homes.

Whether in Paris or our village, we buy most groceries at little shops. The *patisserie* (pah-tis-REE) sells cakes and pastries. We visit a *boulangerie* (boo-LON-zhuh-ree)for breads and a *boucherie* (BOOSH-ree) for meat. A *crémerie* (KREM-uh-ree) sells milk, cheese, yogurt, and butter.

Let's Eat!

When it comes to food, each of our 13 regions has its own cooking style. For example, cooks in Provence, in the south, use lots of garlic, olive oil, and herbs. To the north, cooks in Normandy use a lot of seafood, apples, and butter or cream. Every style offers something delicious. It is all worth a taste!

Most families, including both of ours, always eat together. Sunday lunch is our biggest and most special meal. It consists of soup, roasted meat, and a delicious dessert. During the week, however, lunch is usually smaller than dinner. For breakfast, we have an assortment of breads and drinks. We like to munch on flaky croissants or toast with chocolate-hazelnut spread. Yum! We usually wash it down with a glass of milk or juice.

It is said that we eat more cheese than any other country. We make more than 300 kinds, such as Brie, Camembert, and Roquefort. Try eating cheese with some yummy *baguettes* (bag-EHTS), or "little sticks." These bread loaves can be 3 feet (1 meter) long. In the morning, you might spot people on motor scooters delivering them. But the word "baguettes" doesn't only refer to bread. It is our word for chopsticks and even drumsticks, too!

One dish Chloë and I love is *ratatouille* (rat-ah-TOO-ee). It's a vegetable stew. And you can't go wrong with a pile of *pommes frites* (PAHM FREETS). Those are french fries. For a rare delicacy, try *escargots* (ehs-kar-GOH), which are snails. You can also taste *steak tartare* (STAYK tar-TAR), raw ground beef. There are a lot of options for dessert. Try *tarte tatin* (TAHRT tah-TAN), an upside-down apple pie. Another tasty pastry is the *profiterole* (proh-feet-eh-ROHL). This is a small, round cream puff. If you enjoy custard and caramel, order a delicious *crème brûlée* (KREHM broo-LAY).

Cheese

Escargots

Profiteroles

Crème brûlée

Some schools have class four days a week. Others have classes for five days.

Off to School

Kids often go to a preschool called *la maternelle* (LAH mah-tur-NEHL) from ages 3 to 6. Most of these schools are a half day. Then we go to elementary school until age 11. After that, we attend middle school, called *collège* (koh-LEZH), for four years. That's followed by three years of *lycée* (lee-SAY), or high school. Some students go on to a university, and most are free. One of the most famous universities is the Sorbonne in Paris. It dates back to the 12th century. We both hope to study there.

We currently attend school four days a week. We have Wednesdays off. Many schools in France follow this schedule. School starts at about 8:45 a.m. and ends at 4:00 p.m. Some kids stay until 6:00 p.m. to study or do homework. It sounds like a long day, but we have up to two hours off for lunch and recess.

Math is an important part of our studies in France.

Knowing how to count to 10 is important if you visit France.

1	**un** *(UN)*	6	**six** *(SEES)*
2	**deux** *(DOO)*	7	**sept** *(SET)*
3	**trois** *(TWAH)*	8	**huit** *(WEET)*
4	**quatre** *(KAT-ruh)*	9	**neuf** *(NUHF)*
5	**cinq** *(SANK)*	10	**dix** *(DEES)*

Studying our language, French, is an important part of our education. At one time, French was the international language of business and politics, much like English is today. It was common for educated people around the world, including Thomas Jefferson and Benjamin Franklin, to speak it. The French built settlements, or **colonies**, in many countries around the world. Our language spread through these places, and more than 250 million people speak French today.

In school, we also read a lot of traditional tales. Many were originally shared as spoken stories. Writers such as Charles Perrault later wrote them down. Perrault lived in Paris during the 1600s. His "Tales of Mother Goose" includes stories you might know, such as "Little Red Riding Hood" and "Cinderella." He also wrote "The Ridiculous Wishes."

The Ridiculous Wishes

Once upon a time, there lived a poor woodcutter and his wife. They worked hard but never had much. One day while working, the woodcutter cried, "Why are the gods deaf to my needs and wishes?"

Thunder shook the skies. Suddenly, the god Jupiter appeared. The woodcutter hid in fear. "Do not be afraid," said Jupiter. "You are a hard worker and a good man. I have heard your cries and will grant your first three wishes."

The woodcutter raced home to tell his wife. The two began to dream of all the riches they would wish for. That night, the woodcutter's wife made a fire to warm their tiny hut. The woodcutter relaxed in his chair.

"Oh, how I wish I had a tasty black pudding," he said. Instantly, a black pudding, a sausage made with blood, appeared.

"How dare you waste a wish on a sausage!" screamed the woodcutter's wife. "We could have riches beyond belief."

"How dare you yell at me!" shouted the woodcutter. "I wish this black pudding was hanging from your nose."

A long coil of black pudding appeared on the end of her nose. The woodcutter was horrified. He ran to comfort her. "I have one wish left," he said. "I can wish for riches, but you will live your life with that string of black pudding hanging from your nose. Tell me, dear. Do you want to live unhappily with all these riches? Or, do you want to return to our normal life?"

The woodcutter's wife whispered her decision, and he made his third and final wish. The two lived happily ever after—without pudding on the wife's nose or anything more than what they already had.

The Eiffel Tower sways in the wind almost 5 inches (13 centimeters)!
The Louvre
Mona Lisa

Touring France

Paris: Capital City

Bienvenue (bee-ah-veh-NOO), welcome, to the "City of Lights" and our home, Paris. It's the capital of France. The Eiffel Tower is the tallest building in our city. Almost 7 million people come to visit this structure each year. Visitors can take a rickety elevator ride up to the third level for an amazing view. From there, a person might even spot our apartment building!

Paris is also home to the largest museum in the world, the Louvre. It has the famous painting, the *Mona Lisa*. An Italian artist, Leonardo da Vinci, painted it in 1503. The painting is small. Crowds gather around it to get a good look.

Our city is known for its many cafés. If you need a rest, sit at an outdoor table, sip a hot coffee or cocoa, and watch the people pass by.

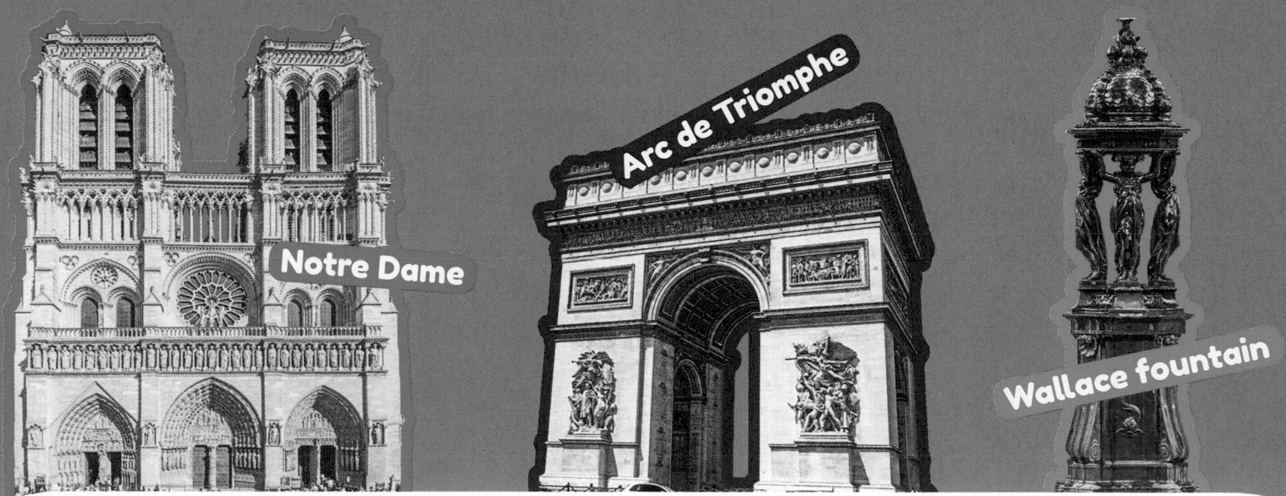

Another must-see spot in Paris is Notre-Dame **Cathedral**. This church sits on an island in the River Seine, which runs through our city. Next, walk under the Arc de Triomphe. This giant stone arch honors our brave soldiers. It stands over the wide Avenue des Champs-Élysées. France's oldest puppet-show theater is also found on this street. Called Guignol, it started about 200 years ago.

People wanting to travel quickly through the city can hop on the Metro, our **subway**, to zip around. It's fast and cheap. Many of the roughly 300 Metro stations are marked with a large letter *M*. Feeling thirsty? Stop for a cool sip of water at a Wallace fountain. They are named after a wealthy Englishman named Sir Richard Wallace. He donated 50 of these drinking fountains to the city in the 1870s.

METROPOLITAIN

Metro entrance

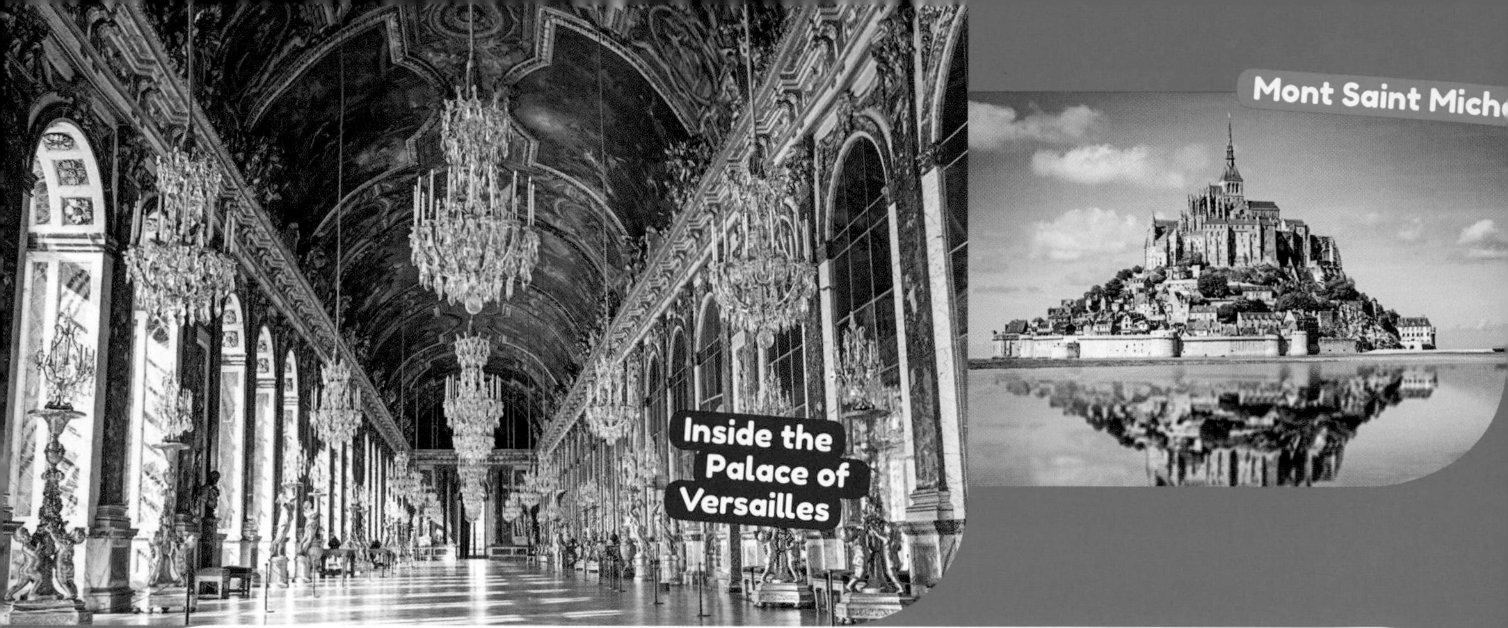

Inside the Palace of Versailles
Mont Saint Miche

Beyond the City

Not far outside of Paris is the magnificent Palace of Versailles. It was built between 1664 and 1682 while Louis XIV was king. The palace was home to several of our rulers, including the famous Queen Marie-Antoinette.

The rest of our country is really interesting, too! In northern France, visit the sites of many major battles from ancient to modern times at places like Normandy. Unusual architecture, such as the island village of Mont Saint Michel, should also not be missed. Surf off the coast of Aquitaine in western France. Or tour ancient Celtic sites in nearby Brittany. The French Riviera, Provence, and other areas of southern France have a lot to offer, too. Lounge on sunny beaches, visit the sea cliffs of the Calanques by boat, wander though fields of lavender, and up into the mountains.

Other Places to Visit

The Alps are France's most majestic mountains. Our families sometimes vacation together in the French Alps. They are home to some of the biggest ski **resorts** in the world. You can ski, snowboard, grab a bowl of hot chocolate, or just enjoy the view. While in the mountains, look for the white peak of Mont Blanc. It is the highest point in the country—and in Europe. It reaches 15,771 feet (4,807 m) into the sky!

The Camargue region is in southeastern France. Fascinating plants and animals, like wild pink flamingos, live in its 300 square miles (777 sq km) of wetlands. Our favorite animals are the small white horses that roam the lands. They are born with brown or black hair, but it turns white as they age.

Flamingo

Our Country's History

Our country has a long and interesting history. People have lived here for about 30,000 years. Celtic groups known as the Gauls settled in the area starting in about the 500s BCE. Rome fought to control the land for many years, and succeeded in the 1st century BCE. In the 400s CE, a tribe called the Franks took over. They ruled for a long time. Our country's name, France, comes from these people.

Timeline: Key Moments in French History

500s BCE

Gauls
Gauls settle across what is now France and parts of Belgium, Italy, and Germany. They spend centuries fighting and interacting with Rome.

400s CE

Franks
Franks, from the Rhine River area, invade Roman territory. Frank king Clovis establishes a Christian kingdom centered in Paris.

768

Emperor Charlemagne
France reaches its peak size. After Charlemagne's death in 814 CE, it is divided into what is now France and Germany.

1789

Revolution
Starting on July 14, 1789, the French people end royal rule when they storm a Paris prison known as the Bastille.

Powerful **monarchs** have dominated our history. One of the best known rulers was Napoleon Bonaparte. He named himself **emperor** in 1804. He tried to expand French lands by taking over other countries. It wasn't until 1870 that France became a **republic** without a monarch. Today, we elect our officials. We are also part of the European Union, in which many countries in Europe work together.

Emperor Napoleon Bonaparte

French flag

European Union flag

1799–1815

Napoleon Bonaparte
Bonaparte takes over France and later declares himself emperor.

19th century

Colonial Power
The French Empire is the second-largest empire in the world. The empire controls land as far away as the Caribbean Sea.

1914–1918, 1939–1945

World Wars
France fights alongside the United States, Great Britain, and other countries in two wars that involve much of the world.

Present day

European Union
France becomes a powerful European country. It is a founding member of the European Union.

It Came From France

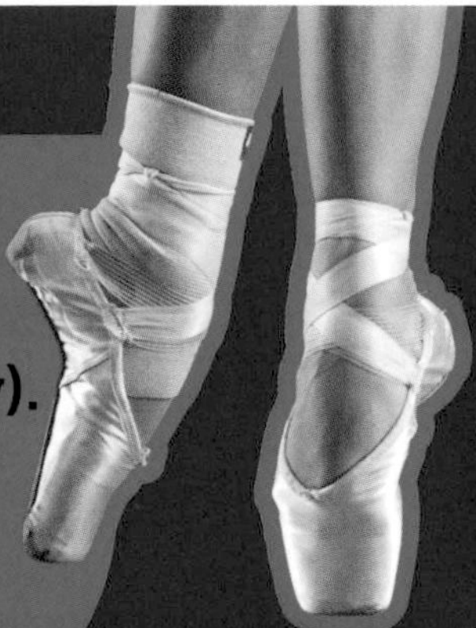

Grab a tutu, point your toes, and *relevé* (RUH-luh-vay). Ballet, as we know it today, began in France in 1832.

French people, young and old, love comics. We have many to choose from. Astérix is a popular comic book series that is also found all over the world. It follows the adventures of two friends, Astérix and Obelix, during the time of the Gauls.

Paris is one of the world's top fashion centers. Many famous designers, such as Coco Chanel and Louis Vuitton, are French. A type of clothing called *haute couture* (OHT koo-TOOR) started here. It is very fancy and super expensive. Designers specially make these clothes to fit their wealthy clients.

As gruesome as it is, the guillotine was invented in France by surgeon Antoine Louis. Louis designed it as a quick and painless way to execute, or kill, prisoners. It worked by cutting off a prisoner's head. Queen Marie-Antoinette and King Louis XVI were beheaded in 1793 during the French Revolution. It was used until 1977.

The French hero Joan of Arc led our troops to victory in a war with England in 1429. In 1431, however, she was captured and burned at the stake. She was later declared a saint. In fact, she's the **patron**, or protecting and guiding, saint of France.

Have you ever seen the Statue of Liberty in New York City? Well, you have us to thank for it. This symbol of the United States was a gift from France in 1886. It celebrated France's aid to the United States in the American Revolution (1775–1783).

Candy shops make chocolate and marzipan fish just for April 1.

Celebrate!

Everyone loves a holiday, and we have some fun ones in France. Our favorite is Poisson d'Avril, or "April Fish." It occurs on April 1. It's a fun day of pranks and practical jokes that started in 1564. If you're here then, be on the lookout. We try all day to tape a paper fish on someone's back, especially on an adult, without being noticed. When they discover that they've been walking around with a paper fish taped to their back all day, we yell "April Fish!" In other parts of the world, this day is known as April Fools' Day.

Epiphany

On Epiphany children share *galette des rois*. Baked inside is a porcelain *fève*, or bean. If you get it in your slice, you can wear the gold paper crown that comes with the cake.

Mardi Gras (le Carnaval)

Parades, colorful costumes, and great music are all a part of the celebration.

Bastille Day

This holiday celebrates the day the French Revolution began and France ended royal rule. Our national colors— blue, white, and red— are everywhere!

Festival de Cornouaille

This festival in Brittany honors our Celtic roots. There are puppet shows, lessons in making lace, wrestling matches, food, and dance.

Make an April Fish

Materials: construction paper (many colors), scissors, circle-shaped color-coding stickers, googly eyes, tape

Step 1 Cut out fish shapes from many different colors of construction paper.

Step 2 Cut each color-coding sticker in half. Use them as “scales” to decorate the fish. Add a googly eye.

Step 3 Add a strip of tape to the top of the fish. You’ll use this to stick the fish on someone’s back.

Step 4 Sneak up on an adult and tape the fish to his or her back without being noticed.

The biker in first place for the day gets to wear the yellow jersey.

Time to Play

SCORE! We French kids love our sports. Soccer is our favorite! Our families and friends gather around the TV whenever our national team plays. The team is known as *Les Bleus* (LAY BLOO), or "The Blues." That's because they wear blue shirts.

Motor racing started in France in 1894. At first, the cars didn't race around a track. They raced between and through our cities. Some motor races, such as the Grand Prix, still work like this. Our other well-known race is a grueling three-week bike race called the Tour de France. Every July, riders cycle a challenging route of more than 2,235 miles (3,597 km) along French roads. The race ends in Paris.

Race car

Fencing is a sword-fighting sport that is also popular. Competitors try to strike each other with the tips of their swords. Fencers wear plenty of protective gear to stay safe.

One of our traditional games from southern France is *boules* (BOOL). You'll spot people playing it in village squares all over the country. It is played using small, metal balls. Each player takes a turn rolling a ball to the *cochonnet* (koh-shoh-NAY), which is a smaller ball. Sometimes you hit another player's ball and push it away. That's the fun part! The player whose ball lands closest to the cochonnet wins. But no pastime is as popular in France as walking. Everyone can enjoy that!

We also like to go horseback riding, play rugby or tennis, ski in the Alps, or sail along the coasts.

You Won't Believe This!

France was the first country to ban supermarkets from throwing away unsold food. The markets must donate unsold foods to food banks or other charities before it goes bad.

France has produced great scientists. Our Marie Curie was the first woman to win a Nobel Prize. She is also the only woman ever to win in two different fields: physics and chemistry.

Two of our famous leaders, King Louis XVI and Emperor Napoleon Bonaparte, suffered from ailurophobia. That's the fear of cats. Meow-wow!

Paris has more than 70 museums. One is devoted to sewers. P.U.! Another explores the Roman-built **catacombs** (pictured) under Paris. Catacombs are underground cemeteries.

French law only allows your pet to travel with you on the TGV, France's high-speed train, if it is small (less than 11 pounds, or 5 kilograms) and has its very own ticket!

The Massif Central, a mountain range in France, is the world's largest collection of extinct volcanoes. It has about 450 of them.

Potatoes were illegal in France in the mid-1700s. People believed growing them caused leprosy, a deadly disease.

France regularly tops the list of tourist destinations! More than 80 million people from all over the world come to our country every year.

The world's first face and artificial heart (pictured) **transplant** surgeries took place in France.

Guessing Game!

Here are some other great sites around France. If you have time, try to see them all!

1. Bayeux Tapestry
2. Cave Paintings in Lascaux and Les Eyzies
3. Centre Georges Pompidou
4. Chartres Cathedral
5. Disneyland Paris
6. Gorges du Verdon
7. Rocamadour Village

A This theme park, which started in the United States, has a site in Paris.

B Known as France's Grand Canyon, this gorge is a must-see.

C One of the oldest and most impressive Gothic cathedrals in the world.

D Tourists flock to this amazing cliffside village in southern France.

E These cave paintings date to 15,000 BCE.

F This cultural center in Paris was built inside out, with pipes and systems on the outside. Blue pipes are for air-conditioning, yellow for electricity, green for water, and red for people.

G This embroidered medieval tapestry is almost 230 feet (70 m) long. It hangs in Bayeux, Normandy, in northern France.

Answer Key

1G, 2E, 3F, 4C, 5A, 6B, 7D

How to Prepare for Your Visit

You might have the chance to see France in person someday. Here are some tips to prepare for a trip.

❶ Our money is called the euro. Many other members of the European Union use euros, too. You'll need them to buy fun souvenirs.

❷ France has special numbers to call in case of emergency. Dial 15 for an ambulance, 17 for the police, 18 for the fire brigade, and 112 for a general emergency. The word for "help" is *au secours* (OH seh-KOOR).

❸ A fast way to travel around our country is on a TGV (Train à Grande Vitesse). TGVs are high-speed trains. There is also the underwater Channel Tunnel that connects France and the United Kingdom.

❹ On most of our public transportation, kids under age 4 travel for free. Kids ages 4 through 11 travel for half price, unless you're in Paris. Then the reduced fee is only for kids ages 4 through 9.

❺ If you feel exhausted after running around, don't worry. Here, people sleep nine hours each day on average. And so should you!

❻ France generally has warm summers and mild winters. Strong, cold winds, known as the *mistral*, blow across the south of France in winter and spring. A hot wind, called the sirocco, brings humidity from the Mediterranean Sea and dust from the Sahara Desert into southern France. Keep this in mind when you pack for your trip.

The United States Compared to France

Official Name	United States of America (USA)	French Republic
Official Language	No official language, though English is most commonly used	French
Population	325 million	67 million
Common Words	yes, no, please, thank you	oui (WEE), non (NOH), s'il vous plaît (SEEL VOO PLAY), merci (mair-SEE)
Flag		
Money	Dollar	Euro
Location	North America	Western Europe
Highest Point	Denali (Mount McKinley)	Mont Blanc
Lowest Point	Death Valley	Sea level, along the coast
National Anthem	"The Star-Spangled Banner"	"La Marseillaise"

So now you know some important and fascinating things about our country, France. We hope to see you someday taking photos of the Eiffel Tower, sipping hot chocolate in a café, or relaxing on one of our southern beaches. Until then . . . *au revoir* (OH reh-VWAH).

Glossary

catacombs *(KAT-uh-cohmz)* cemeteries located underground

cathedral *(kuh-THEE-druhl)* a large and important church

colonies *(KAH-luh-neez)* territories that have been settled by people from another country and are controlled by that country

emperor *(EM-pur-ur)* the ruler of an empire

monarchs *(MAH-nurks)* people who rule a country, such as a king or queen

patron *(PAY-truhn)* a type of saint believed to look after an individual, group of people, a particular activity, a city, or a country

republic *(rih-PUHB-lik)* a form of government in which people have the power to elect representatives who manage the government

resorts *(rih-ZORTS)* places where people go for rest and recreation

subway *(SUHB-way)* an electric train or system of trains that runs underground in a city

transplant *(TRANS-plant)* a medical operation in which a damaged organ is replaced by a healthy one

Index

Facts for Now

Visit this Scholastic website for more information on France and to download the Teaching Guide for this series:

www.factsfornow.scholastic.com Enter the keyword **France**

About the Author

Wiley Blevins lives and works in New York City. His greatest love is traveling, and he has been all over the world, including France. He has also written the Ick and Crud series and the Scary Tales Retold series.